RICH MASKEY

FAMILY DOG

The Ultimate Guide On Caring For Your Family Dog, Learn The Essentials and Useful Tips You Need to Take Perfect Care Of Your Dog

Descrierea CIP a Bibliotecii Naţionale a României
RICH MASKEY
    FAMILY DOG. The Ultimate Guide On Caring For Your Family Dog, Learn The Essentials and Useful Tips You Need to Take Perfect Care Of Your Dog / Rich Maskey. – Bucharest: Editura My Ebook, 2020
    ISBN

RICH MASKEY

FAMILY DOG

The Ultimate Guide On Caring For Your Family Dog, Learn The Essentials and Useful Tips You Need to Take Perfect Care Of Your Dog

My Ebook Publishing House
Bucharest, 2020

RICH MASKEY

FAMILY DOG

The Ultimate Guide On Caring For Your Family Dog
Learn The Essentials and Useful Tips You Need to Take
Perfect Care Of Your Dog

My Book Publishing House
Richmond 2022

TABLE OF CONTENT

INTRODUCTORY

Need A Little Help with Your Health? Get A Dog! Dogs are considered man's best friend. But did you know that having a dog gives you several health benefits?

In studies done by medical professionals, dog owners benefit from their pet's presence in several ways:

1. Improved cardiovascular health - Dog owners have been proven to have blood pressure and cholesterol lower than ordinary people. These factors reduce the chance for cardiovascular diseases. Stroking a pet has long been known to reduce blood pressure.

A study from the New York State University found that these benefits continue even without the pet available. The study tested a group of stockbrokers with hypertension. They concluded that just being a pet-owner can lower blood pressure.

Dog owners also have blood cholesterol levels lower than normal. Five thousand four hundred people were tested by the Baker Medical Research Institute of Australia and with the results showing pet owners having not just lower blood pressure but also lower levels of blood triglycerides and cholesterol compared to people who didn't own any pets.

2. Faster recovery time and higher survival rates - Hospital studies have found that seniors and recently operated on patients responded better to treatment and got better quickly while they were in contact with dogs and other therapy animals. Just petting a dog can be relaxing and therapeutic for recovering patients.

Also, dog owners have a greater chance to survive after suffering from a serious illness. Several studies have discovered that pet owners who suffered from a heart attack were more likely to be alive a year after they were discharged from the hospital than those who did not own pets.

Another New York study found that pets affected their survival rate more even more than the presence or company of family members or friends.

3. Fewer visits to the doctor - Studies conducted at Cambridge and UCLA have found that owning a pet corresponds to overall improved health and less need for hospital visits. A Medicare study of its elderly patients also discovered that those who own dogs visit the doctor less than those who don't have a pet.

4. Mental Wellness - Patients who have dogs have also been known to have better emotional health than their counterparts. They offer unconditional love and affection; their presence alone helps reduce loneliness for sick people who have otherwise been isolated. Several studies of people with major illnesses have shown that the stress of fighting the disease is significantly reduced when they had a dog as company.

As you can see, having a dog is a great investment, for the joy that you get from owning one and the health benefits that you can receive. So, go out and get a dog!

CHAPTER 1

WHAT PEOPLE NEED TO KNOW
ABOUT DOG BEHAVIOR

**As the old adage goes, "Dogs are man's best friend."
However, there are times when people just can't understand
why their beloved dogs behave in a different manner.**

Hence, it is extremely important to know the underlying
reasons why dogs sometimes behave differently.

You can teach your dog appropriate behavior. Experts say
that dog behaviors can be controlled through proper training.

Dog behaviors are actually responses that are mostly
triggered by environmental and social factors. Hence, to control
these responses, the owner should teach his dogs the proper way
to respond to such elements. Let's explore a few of the methods:

Dog Bite

Statistics show that almost 5 million people in the U.S. are victims of dog bites annually. This is almost 2% of the total population in the U.S. What's more, dog bites cases rank as second most common cause of emergencies in the hospitals.

So, the question is: Why dogs bite?

According to the experts, the main reasons why dogs may bite are the following:

1. Excitement

When somebody plays with his or her dog, the tendency of the dog is to get excited, and because dogs don't have hands to use when playing, they use their mouth to grasp things. When this happens, there is the tendency that the dog might accidentally hurt people without intending to do anything harmful.

2. Protection

Dogs can be very possessive, so, whenever he wants to protect something that he owns, he will bite whoever threatens to take it away from him.

Hence, when people get near the dog's property, the dog's tendency is to bite to make the person leave his property alone.

3. Pain

When the dog is not feeling well, he does not understand why he is feeling that way. Therefore, when a person, even if it's his master, touches him, he may think that it's the person who causes the pain and so his tendency is to fight back by biting.

4. Fear

Dogs are sometimes afraid just like humans. That is why when somebody startles him, the dog's only known protection for itself is to bite back.

The best thing is to avoid these situations and leave the dog alone. The problem with so many people is that they want to always play around with their dog without learning how and when the dogs should be left alone.

Like humans, dogs have feelings too. When these feelings are all mixed up, their only known protection for themselves is to bite because they cannot understand the situation logically. Therefore, people should know that in order to avoid such circumstances.

CHAPTER 2

DOGS DURING LABOR

Breeding dogs is an exciting experience. From the time a proper mate is found to the point that the puppies are born, it is crucial to take careful steps to make this successful.

Professional breeders do not breed frequently and will only do so when a pair is found to be healthy that will ensure the birth of healthy offspring.

The ideal breeder should have the pair of dogs tested for every possible disease as well as have all the information regarding the pair's ancestors and health records on file. Should a breeder find no problem in the history of the pair, then the process can begin.

Dogs normally come into heat twice a year which is every six months. Larger dogs can come into heat every eight or ten months which usually lasts about three weeks. Vaginal bleeding is a sure sign that the dog is in heat as well as swelling in the vulva. A dog's pregnancy or gestation period lasts between 60 to 67 days. Most dogs give birth after 63 days.

The only way to determine the stage of the dog's pregnancy is by keeping track of time from the day of the breeding. Keeping a record of this on file is advisable for reference purposes.

Exactly three weeks after breeding, the mother must be examined to confirm the pregnancy.

The dog must be given a formulated and premium brand of dog food for the duration of the pregnancy and throughout the nursing period preferably with a strong nutritional foundation.

During pregnancy, the mother's food consumption will almost double have compared to the pre-pregnancy level so increased feeding must be given to ensure that there is enough for both the mother and the puppies.

Behavioral changes are to be expected during this time. The dog will demand far more affection or may experience a few days of vomiting.

Later on, the expectant mother will search for a secure place to deliver the puppies. Ensure that a proper place is ready when the time comes. An ideal place for an expecting mother is a box. Depending on the size of the dog, it must be spacious enough for the dog to move around and must have layers of newspaper inside it that will absorb birthing fluids.

This should also have low sides for the mother to look outside and for the breeder to easily check if assistance is needed to make it easy to remove soiled papers without interrupting the mother and the newborn puppies.

Follow these steps and you should be able to count on a happy birthing process!

CHAPTER 3

WHEN YOUR BEST FRIEND GETS LOST –
TIPS IN FINDING YOUR DOG

"The dog is man's best friend," so the saying goes. Dogs have proven to be loving and loyal companions of people.

From pit bulls to dachshunds to terriers, dogs are a part of daily life.

But what happens when your pet dog gets lost? What if, one day, while you are strolling across a park quite far from home with your Labrador and your pet suddenly gets lost? Do not resort to panic, as this will not help solve the situation.

The first rule when you're going out with your pet dog is never letting it out of sight. In short, do not let your dog get lost. Sometimes there is no avoiding a situation like this. Even dogs that are properly trained will look for ways to be free to roam around.

Here are some ways to find your dog if he is lost:

- Check the various animal shelters in town. If your dog has not been claimed by others or picked up, leave a complete description of your dog with the animal shelter staff. Include your name and contact information. If possible, show a recent photograph of you and your dog. This is also a reason why the license for your pet should be current and updated.

- Check all the pet shops and veterinarians in your vicinity. You could ask the staff or vet if somebody has reported a lost dog and if the dog shares the same characteristics of your lost dog.

- Post details of your dog along with your contact information in billboards or in areas where the dog might have gotten lost.

- If possible, place an ad in the local papers for your lost dog. Also check the "Lost and Found" classifieds.

Check it daily. You'll never know when somebody turns up to say that he or she found your dog.

- Check in your neighborhood. Your dog could be somewhere near. Dogs usually do not stray far from their own homes.

- It would be easier and faster to find the dog if it has complete identification details, such as a name tag, identifiable collar, among others.

- Be sure you have your dog's current photo. Keep it at all times, just in case you need to show what your dog looks like.

Here is one last option to keep in mind. The latest thing in tracking your pet is to have an electronic chip placed just under the skin. The chip contains all the information about your dog and yourself so that the information can be scanned by a vet or a local animal shelter.

Taking care of your dog is like taking care of a dear friend. Show your concern to the dog, and it will return the favor.

CHAPTER 4

THE NAMING GAME

If "fashionistas" are obsessed with brand names, some dog lovers are hooked on dog breeds. This is because purebred dogs are expensive and belong to the higher level of this particular species.

Generally, dog breeds were incorporated to give distinctive characteristics to certain classifications, thus, resulting in a substantial number of varieties.

However, people who breed dogs often find it hard to detect the specific characteristic of the resulting species. There are times that offspring appear to be different from their "parents."

In dog breeding, experts contend that the offspring should have the same characteristics as their parents, both physical attributes and behavior. For example, a breeding pair of Retrievers should produce the black puppies because purebred Retrievers have black coats.

However, there are instances that retrievers produce puppies that have yellow coats. Hence, cases like this are not considered by the known Kennel clubs. What happens next is that these yellow retrievers are sometimes "euthanized" by dog breeders based on the notion that they want to curb the probable reoccurrence of such species.

This particular issue has long been debated by many dog experts and scientists because of the fact that there are certain instances wherein genetic consequences may intervene.

In addition, studies show that dog breeds, like the human race, have no specific scientific origins and that their breeds cannot even be identified and proven even by DNA. So, the chances of getting a purebred dog are not that common.

However, because of the existence of dog breeds, Kennel clubs only consider pure dog breeds on their competitions.

Today, there are about 160 dog breeds being recognized by the club, but most people can only recognize a dozen or two. In fact, even those who are experts in dog breeding may still confuse a certain breed as a cross between two dog breeds.

Hence, dog breeds should not be considered as a basis on whether or not a certain dog will bite. Most people have this thinking that there are dog breeds that will not bite.

People should keep in mind that dog biting is based on behavior, in which certain environmental and social variables trigger the behavior. Hence, experts contend that there is no breed of dog that will attack somebody without any reason at all. This means that 99.9% of all dogs will not attack anyone as long as there are no viable reasons that will trigger the attack.

The bottom line is that dog breeds may still vary, depending on their genetic make-up. Hence, the foundation of classifying dogs according to their physical attributes and behavior may be affected by different factors.

It isn't any wonder why the issues about purebreds are endless!

CHAPTER 5

PREVENTING YOUR DOG
FROM CATCHING DISEASES

Like any other pet, dogs, if not properly cared for and maintained, can get diseases.

Here are some parasites that cause dog diseases.

Heartworm. Mosquito bites cause heartworm to exist in a dog and will reside in your pet's heart and nearby blood vessels. A dog infected by heartworms looks dull and may even have a chronic cough. If possible, ask your veterinarian if your dog could be given a heartworm medication when it is the season of mosquitoes.

Hookworm. Hookworms can be given by the mother dog to a puppy during the nursing period or even before birth. Hookworms cause dog anemia and appetite loss.

Roundworm. The transmittal of roundworms is very much like how hookworms get transmitted in a dog. An infected dog usually has a potbelly. Roundworms cause pneumonia, diarrhea, dehydration, stunted growth, and vomiting.

Tapeworm. A dog gets tapeworms if it swallows fleas that are larvae-laden. Much of the symptoms that are obvious rarely show, but in the dog's feces, you could see deposits of a rice-like appearance.

Whipworm. A dog infected with whipworms may have diarrhea and other ailments like, stool mucus, and serious bowel inflammation. Extreme weight loss is also a symptom caused by whipworms.

Fleas. Fleas, the commonest among external parasites, cause the dog to continuously scratch various parts of the body. This results to fur loss. Ask your veterinarian on a good flea-control program, since fleas could become resistant to some products over time.

Lice. Lice can infect less common compared with fleas. Plus, they can be controlled easier.

Ticks. Ticks can pose more serious problems than fleas because diseases like Rocky Mountain Spotted Fever, or Lyme disease, can be contracted with ticks. Tweezers can be used to remove ticks one by one. If you do not know how to remove ticks properly and carefully, ask your vet first. If you do know how, ticks should be placed in a can with soap and water.

Treating dog diseases

Some ways of treating dog diseases that your vet might use:

- Pills
- Liquid medicine
- Eye drops and ointment
- Ear drops and ointment

With proper care and prevention, your pet dog will be generally free and safe from various diseases. If you notice something's wrong with your dog or he is acting strangly, immediately consult with your vet.

CHAPTER 6

TIPS FOR BUYING DOG FOOD

It is not enough for dogs to have a full stomach after every meal. Besides a non-sedentary lifestyle, pets need proper nutrition in order to be healthy, happy and their coats soft and glossy.

The cost of dog food and its brand is only important if dogs can read or pay for his meal. The easiest and best way to find out which food is best for man's best friend is to observe how their response is to the chow they take in.

The following are tips that one should remember in feeding dog any kibbles, nibbles or whatever kinds of treats.

- **Chocolate is lethal to dogs.**

Specifically, the dark chocolate kind. The major components methylxanthine alkaloids and theobromine in regular chocolate is digested & excreted by humans in as little as 3 hours but the same compounds when ingested by dogs stays inside them for 18 hours. This has been proven to be fatal.

Symptoms of chocolate dog poisoning include vomiting, excessive urination, hyperactivity, diarrhea, followed by seizure, coma, and death.

- **Read the label.**

Dogs should have a diet rich in meat protein. When purchasing canned foods, look for chicken, turkey meat, pork or other animal by products as these keep the dog's coat smooth and healthy. Dogs prefer foods which contain high vegetable protein levels because these are easily digestible and are a great source of energy.

- **Don't give a dog a bone!**

Contrary to the popular nursery song, feeding bones to dogs is not a good idea. Small soft bones gnawed and eaten by dogs feel like splinters inside their throat causing them to choke. Remember, dogs have short digestive tracts. They also have no saliva amylase, an enzyme that is used to pre- digest starch.

- **Dog food supplements are unnecessary...**

...only if one is sure that their dog receives a regular intake of complete and balanced food nutrients. Good sources of carbohydrates include rice, corn, oatmeal, wheat. However, a highly specialized nutrition is only necessary if dogs do not get enough physical activity or are currently undergoing a stressful routine change.

- **Raw fish and eggs are a no-no.**

Consistent consumption of raw eggs makes a dog's skin breakout. In canine terms - since eggs diminish the biotin available in their body – dermatitis and hair loss are its usual effects. Raw fish meanwhile results in thiamine- deficiency in a dog. Its effects usually are loss of appetite, abnormal posture, weakness and in some cases death.

Feed your dog a healthy diet and he will return the favor with a beautiful coat and many years of companionship!

CHAPTER 7

ESSENTIAL CARE TIPS FOR YOUR DOG

Dogs are loving pets. But caring for them is a bit of hard work.

Here are some tips to consider in taking care of your dog:

If you do not have a dog yet, consider the area where your dog can exercise. If you have a big yard where you could exercise or play with your dog, you might want to get a large dog such as a German Shepherd, Labrador, or Golden Retriever. If you have a smaller space, get a smaller dog like a Terrier or Dachshund. These types of dogs need little exercise compared with the larger dogs.

You also need to consider your dog if there are children in your house. Some dogs like Pit bulls and Dalmatians are sometimes temperamental.

It is important that you groom your dog. A regular groom is recommended. Dog's ears should be cleaned, with the wax and dirt removed every week. Ear cleaning also helps you detect presence of ear mites or infections. The dog should be bathed weekly with warm water and dog shampoo.

It is also recommended that you brush your dog at least once a week.

After grooming your pet, do take it to a veterinarian to get its anti-rabies shots and over-all checkup.

A diet that is balanced and nutritious is recommended for your dog. Contrary to what many people think, dogs do not just eat meat. They also need carbohydrates. A diet consisting of 50 percent of protein or meat and 50 percent of carbohydrates is the preferred diet for dogs.

As implied earlier, dogs need some amount exercise. Aside from their health, dogs exercising will prevent them from retrieving and chasing, digging, and chewing on various things. Exercises depend on your dog's sex, age, and health level. A dog likes to jog, fetch, and race-walk a lot. One warning however, start slow in exercising your dog. Unfortunately, some dogs enjoy themselves so much when they do these exercises. They do not know when to stop it.

Having a dog to last you for a long time does not end with just owning one. You have to take care of it. Although that may be hard work, it will also bring you fun and enjoyment when you see that your dog is healthy and loves you. Having a pet dog of your own is a pleasurable experience.

CHAPTER 8

FIVE SIMPLE TIPS TO GET YOUR DOG
READY FOR DOG SHOWS

Every truly avid dog owner wishes for the chance to show off his pet at the nearest dog show.

It is both a way to validate your pride in owning your pet and a chance to see other beautiful dogs in action. For the first timer, however, entering the world of competitive dog shows can truly be a daunting experience.

Here are five simple tips to get your dog, and yourself, ready for the limelight:

1. Know The Field - Everybody has to start somewhere and entering dog shows requires that you know what to expect. Read literature on dog shows. Go to dog shows as a spectator and see what goes on. Get a good grasp of the jargon. Knowing the difference between all-breed dog shows and specialty shows can help a lot in determining what shows to join and how to get your pet ready.

2. Know Your Dog - Knowledge of your pet is essential when getting ready for a dog show. A little effort in researching your dog's breed and health history can pay off immensely. Getting familiar with your dog's quirks, habits and abilities is also a great way to bond with them and paves the way to a successful performance in the show ring.

3. Training, Lots of Training - Training for the show, for yourself and your dog is very important. It is advisable that you have the help of a trained handler when you're starting out. Training dogs also requires conditioning them physically so that they are in tip-top shape when they participate in the show. Remember, dog shows are like beauty pageants. A well-trained dog is both pleasant to look at and be with.

4. A Visit To The Vet - Every dog needs a visit to the vet when getting ready for a dog show. Having your pet inoculated is a standard procedure to protect your dog, and other dogs, from spreading diseases during the show.

A check-up on your pet's physical condition would also help greatly in assuring that your pride and joy is ready for the show.

5. Ask Questions - Learning is a continual process. Asking questions from handlers and veterinarians on how you should treat or handle your dog can open up insights on caring for it.

These five simple tips are just the beginning. Like they say, experience is the best teacher, but with this advice you're well on your way to getting your dog ready for the show.

Basic Principles in a Dog Lovers Club

There are lots of dog lover's clubs in the US that offer a lot more for both the dog lovers and their dogs. Here are some of them.

The American Kennel Club has a dog lovers section called "For the Love of the Purebred Dog". This article is more than a canine purebred section. It is dedicated to living at home with dogs. This dog club gives informative and educational materials pertaining to pet care, training, nutrition and a lot more. It also includes funny stories, art, pet history and the more popular Companion Animal Recovery method. There are also more popular sites like the dog breeds and events page.

The American Mixed Breed Obedience Registration or (AMBOR) on the other hand was created in 1983 with the objective of taking into accounts the perseverance and accolades in obedience contests of mix breed dogs and handlers. This dog lovers club also gives support and inspiration to dog handlers.

Important Information for Members:

1. Mixed-breeds

Unlimited full membership is open to handlers and owners of mixed-breed dogs as long as the pet is spayed and nails are cut. There should be front and side photo shots of the dog that will be included in the application. This is the ticket to all the obedience and agility programs, automatic tabulation in the agility and obedience nationwide ranking system. This also includes a given eligibility for the annual awards.

This achievement will be given honor in AMBOR highlights (AMBOR'S newsletter) and on the website. The member will be eligible to any agility and obedience national competition in the future. Dogs with assigned numbers are marked as purebred and should be enlisted as a purebred. Also, dogs that are listed as mixed-breeds that are given a number based on the owner's application causes its membership to be changed to a status of a purebred.

2. Purebreds

Purebred dogs can be listed with AMBOR with a rule that entry is limited to the AMBOR-supported agility program. All dogs that are purebred, listed with AMBOR and exhibits AMBOR-supported programs on agility will have competition points monitored and there will be an automatic issuance of certificates.

Dogs that are purebred and listed with AMBOR are not qualified to be a part of the agility and obedience scoring systems. They will also not be included in the website on highlights and not qualified for any mixed-breeds national competition in the future.

Handlers that register to the AMBOR-supported trials on agility should put their AMBOR number on the form at the club's entrance so that competition points will be monitored.

CHAPTER 9

ADOPTING A DOG – PUPPY OR ADULT?

Everyone is surely going to get excited when trying to adopt a dog. Truly a man's best friend, you can rely on your pet dog in giving you company, cuddling up together and some can even guard your house.

You need to review your personal lifestyle and needs when adopting a dog. It is a major decision whether or not you would choose to have a puppy or an adult as a pet. Before deciding on which dog to adopt, here is some useful information that might help you decide.

On Puppies

- Bringing up a puppy is an advantage because this means that you would guide its growth and wellbeing. You would have the chance to raise it up according to what you want. This means you can ensure that it is properly nurtured with the right dog food, ensure that necessary dog shots are given and prevent heartworm at this early stage. Having your puppy personally trained is also a plus since you can teach him exactly what you want.

- You should adopt a puppy when it is at least 10 weeks old. Puppies need a lot of time to be cared for by their mothers. This is a crucial stage for them. They somehow gain a psychological advantage for both puppy and for the mother dog as well.

- A puppy can easily adjust to new surroundings as compared to an adult dog. Although most puppies may cause minimal to major damage to your personal stuff while they are in the stage of teething. They need to be housebroken and house training needs a lot of time, effort and patience from the owner.

- There is no assurance of what a puppy would look like when it gets old; especially if it is a mixed breed. Also, his temperament might change when he grows up.

- Most pet owners love how puppies can be entertaining. They are very cute and adorable pets that is a hit for both children and grownups. Puppies can be easily regarded as one of the family.

On adult dog

- You would have less of a fuss taking care of an adult dog. They already have this established behavior that you can easily adopt too. By being with the dog more often, you would have more or less an idea of what its temperament is.

- You need to get as much information that you can when adopting an adult dog. Take note of its habits and mood swings. You can acquire information from the previous owners of the dog. Some adult dogs may have some behavior issues. It is important to take note of them.

- It may take some time and effort for an adult dog to be completely comfortable with a new owner.

- Take note that you need to introduce an adult dog to your children and other household members. This would help the dog be familiar with them and helps them refrain from biting or barking thinking that they maybe strangers.

- Adult dogs may not need your full attention unlike puppies need and would require lesser trips to the veterinary.

- For a fully-grown dog physique and behavior is basically not a variable anymore. What you see is basically what you get.

- Most dogs are housebroken already so they would cause lesser damage to your belongings and don't wake up at night like most puppies do. Usually, they have grown out of the impulse of chewing things.

- An older dog can easily adapt to other pets, like other dogs or cats, if you have a group of them at your household.

Adopting a dog is not an easy task and choosing which one to adopt can be a little tricky too. Everyone loves sweet looking puppies, but not everyone can stand up to the tiresome house training. Though most would appreciate the bonding shared with them.

Adult dogs need no great amount of guidance but can still turn out to be a lovable pet. Whichever you think is the right pet for you, just keep in mind that taking care of them requires a lot of time and effort. In return, they would always keep you company and has ready smile with an excited wag of tail waiting for you everyday.

9 786069 836460

Printed by Libri Plureos GmbH in Hamburg, Germany